Beauty V/S Beast

A Tale of Survival

Prarena Mirchandani

Made with ❤ on the BookLeaf Publishing Platform
www.bookleafpub.in
www.bookleafpub.com

Dedication

To all those who have survived the darkest of
times

Acknowledgement

I am deeply grateful to those who have supported and inspired me throughout my journey of writing this book. First and foremost, I want to thank my family—my mother, Neelam Mirchandani, whose unwavering love and wisdom have shaped me into the person I am today. My brother, Krishna Mirchandani, has been a constant source of encouragement and joy, always reminding me to stay grounded and focused. To my father, Vishnu Mirchandani, whose guidance and strength have been the foundation of my resilience, thank you for always believing in me.

I also extend my heartfelt gratitude to Shree Radharani and Shree Krishna, whose divine presence and grace have gifted me the ability to process even the most traumatic experiences through the art of poetry. It is through this sacred connection that I have found the strength to express and transform my deepest emotions. Without this profound inspiration, this book would not have been possible.

To all who have walked beside me on this journey, your support has been invaluable, and I dedicate this work to you with all my heart.

Preface

The words within these pages are not just ink on paper—they are the raw and unfiltered emotions of a young soul navigating through life. This book is a journey of reflection, pain, resilience, and growth. The poems explore the tender spaces where innocence and harsh reality collide, where the sweetness of childhood is tainted by the complexities of the world.

From the heartache of betrayal and confusion to the moments of quiet introspection, the poems capture a deeply personal yet universal experience. The innocent dreams of childhood, where imagination soared freely, are often overshadowed by the sudden weight of society's expectations, the struggles of identity, and the inevitable loss of innocence. Yet, within these struggles, there is a voice—often silenced, but always strong enough to break free.

The collection speaks of growing up, but not in the traditional sense. It's about the loss of simplicity, the confrontation with pain, and the rediscovery of self-worth. Each poem is a battle fought in silence, a cry for understanding, and a plea for healing. Yet, despite the heavy themes, there is always a glimmer of hope, a reminder that the ability to feel, to heal, and to rise again is what truly defines us.

As you turn these pages, you may find fragments of your own story woven within the lines. This book is not just a collection of poems—it is a mirror, reflecting the struggles, joys, and deep emotions of the human experience. It is a conversation between the past and the present, a dialogue with the child within us all, urging us to remember the importance of self-love, empathy, and resilience.

May you find solace, understanding, and courage in these verses.

Mess All Around

Mess is all we see around
Often find ourselves searching for the real
ground

Real and fake all seems the same,
Cuz nobody knows who's what they claim

Too tired to prove anything to anyone,
Does anyone know who has remained the
same

Words and lines stopped making sense,
Rhymes are just left to defense

Abuse Assault, and Aggression are now
common words
Every feeling is ready to kill me like swords

Dear Childhood

Aaj pata nahi kyu likh rahi hu,
Dil me ek ghav ban gaya hai shayad use sil
rahi hu

Ek ladki ki pehchaan uske charitra hoti hai
esa T.V me dekha tha,
Par meri zindagi me physics chemistry se
badhkar na koi bhi jhamela tha

Apni choti si duniya me apni gudiyo se khel
rahi thi,
Tabhi ek hadse se ne sikhaya ki shyd ab mai
badi ho rahi thi

Apne aap ko bold dikhane ke liye mene
ladkiyo ke sare shauk chod diye,
Par pata na tha ki duniya ne meri taraf apne
germanzooriyon ke chehre mod diye

Abhi abhi hi to mene apne aansuo ko
chupana tha seekha,
Pata nahi tha zindagi dikhaegi mujhe dard me
hasne ka bhi tareeka

Pehle to chot lagne par rona aur chocolate par
khush hona aata tha,
Ab zindagi ne mere sath ek alag hi khel khela
tha

Mere pyare se bachpan par ek haiwan ne
nazar daldi,
Un hasi ki kilkariyo ko hasi dabakar izzat ki
zimmedari pakdadi

Ab wo bachpan muskurana bhool chuka hai
Wo chot lagne par rona bhool chuka hai
Wo dekh chuka hai dard ko
Wo khushiyo se mulakatein bhool chuka hai

To bas yahi kehna chahungi,
MY DEAR CHILDHOOD, LET'S BREAK
UP

Scars Wouldn't

Blood and Scars everywhere
I saw things that I couldn't bear
I was told it'll get better
But I couldn't stop my eyes from getting
wetter

I closed my eyes and shut my ears
But everything was too loud not to hear

I still pretended that I didn't feel it
But blood and scars still could scream it

Why do we pretend that our mind has
forgotten
When we know that our body will never let
our soul forget

I still know it is there when I close my eyes
I guess the scars on your soul never let you
forget

Not Feeling Good

Weird people sarcastic smiles
How does one understand allies

"Hey, you're such a good child"
I had BPD and Depression on files

"Extremist, Emotional Bitch you just lie"
Probably not what a teenager should come by

Intrusive melancholia bruises away shy
Weeping traces flesh's whispers but don't pry

Weird people with fake smiles
How does one cope with all those ties

I was bruised I was broken
Still people come to observe with a token

I screamed and screamed but all the gems
were molten

Weird society with dramatic lies
Let's just wait but then everything dies

THAT LIL GIRL IS INTERNALISING IT

You're Insane, You're Bitch
You're wolf, You're Villain

STOP IT, that lil girl is internalising it

You hate her?
Screw you and your fucking opinion like shit

It doesn't give you the right to break her
heart even a bit
She still hasn't seen the world, no need to
push the opinion of it

STOP those harsh words, that lil girl is
internalising it

How much do you eat?
You fat lil shit
What? You don't eat?
You look like a matchstick

Your hair are so curly, they look like chidiya
ka ghosla
Stop that kainchi si zubaan, who's gonna
marry you lil shit

PLEASE STOP YOU SHITTY PEOPLE
THAT LIL GIRL IS INTERNALISING IT

Hazy Crazy

In the messy thoughts
In the pain that was caught

Nobody knew how I was, My emotions were
left to rot
There were times when I was taught, your
pain and emotions are a lot

I didn't agree, I kept quiet
Oh god! I didn't know I wasn't alright
I smiled and smiled cuz that's what you're
supposed to do, right??

Then one day that smile broke
Body shivered and panic stroke
I couldn't pretend anymore

I don't know now, What is pretend, What is
not
It has become like a blurred spot
I don't know who I am anymore
Is it real or is it just a crazy thought?

Pretty Thoughts

Pretty thoughts and Pretty smiles
Doesn't come without a web of lies

Blinded eyes and Dreamy skies
No one likes saying goodbyes

It's okay if it's not alright
Everyday doesn't have to be sunny and bright

Sky is purple and the air is pink
Only if you could love yourself from within

Your feelings are your way to heal
Let's feel, heal and don't forget to have a
proper meal

I'M Not The One (For You)

Dream of one or Dream of none
Turn around, why can't I be the one?

I tried and cried
But all the love had dried
Who am I to have had a say.?
When I was not the one for which he prayed

Did you see the turn?
You're not the one

I wrote letters in the skies,
But all the promises turned out to be lies
Painted my dream on our love canvas,
But you tore it down with a shattered glass

Broken heart or broken glass
You stopped the story in between the trance

Dream of turn or Dream of burn

The visions turned out to be bad omens

Who am I to ignore the signs
So, I stopped reading between the lines
When I removed the reds which were turning
me blind
Saw you with a knife in my heart, and you
were not kind

Let's work on things that do align with my
aura and sun
I'm the love of my life and not the other one

Dream of one or Dream of none
Let's accept I'm not the one (for you)

Uss Bachhi Ne Socha Hoga

Sone ka samay aur panchtantra ki kahaniya
pyari
Shyd is baar sapne me mjhe safed Hans aur
dikhe ek kyari
Us bacchi ne socha hoga

Raat ke andhere me jab nindiya Rani aati hai
Pyare Pyare sapne de kuch khushiya bhi dejati
h
Us raat me ye kya horha hai, kyu koi mjhe yun
jhakjor Raha hai
Us bacchi ne socha hoga

Nindiya Rani nahi aayi
Raat jab hogayi thi bilkul kaali syahi
Khauf aur ghabrahat ne mjhe samet liya
Cheekhna Chillana us din kaam nahi kiya
Uss bacchi ne socha hoga

Pariya achhi hoti hai

Sabki suraksha karti hai
Fir mere liye koi pari kyu nahi hai
Kyu mjhe wnha tadapne diya
Kyu wo dard sehne diya
Us bacchi ne socha hoga

Insaan ki haiwaniyat dekhkar
Us din Ishwar bhi chaukh gaya
Nindiya Rani bhi kaanp gayi,
Pariya Puri raat royi
Ab pata na tha ki kab saaf insaaf hoga
Uss raat us bacchi ki pukar sunkar, Ishwar ne
apani banayi duniya ke astitva ko kosa hoga

While Writing

Inspiration comes in many ways
Especially if it is one of those rainy days

Sprinkler splashes between the maize
The desire to acquire wasn't raised

Conflicting notions were sought
In the field of war were they brought
Freaking fun I was they thought
But finally the paradigm shift took place

Dedication comes in many ways
Especially if it is one of those crazy days

Friction destruction with crusty strays
Restriction construction still leaves us amaze

Screaming Nights

Loud screams at 10 AM sight
Kept my ears and eyes shut tight

Moment by Moment, second by second
I knew at the time nothing was alright

Inhaled exhaled but the air was light
I haven't slept after that particular night

Next day was school, I was up and quiet
Heard hollow vows broken after a few
daylights

Constantly pretended to exist out of fright
A part of my soul stood at the terrace height

She didn't jump but now I feel I might
Intentions of crowd did not look very bright

Numbing void, atleast I wasn't dead right?
But the concept looked blurred of fair fight

Crowd manipulated heart to be against mind

She stayed back leaving factual insights

Love isn't Fear

When love is fear
And fear is love
Every story doesn't fit like the perfect glove

Who's lying and who's saying the truth
Your inner child or your so-called beloved

I can identify them with just the sound of
footsteps
The dark circle marked by the four-leaved
clove

Screaming shadows identified as love
Blood ties established
Peaceful / loving is not only represented by
love

I cried myself to sleep until I was completely
lost
People kept saying I matured early maybe
that was the cost
She's such an innocent child, we never see her
exhaust

Marks on her body screeched she felt crossed

Know the scariest part of this poetry tossed?
From love to fear and fear to love,
It was a truth lived and felt, all of the above

Morning Scribbles

What is peace and calm, asked by you
4 AM mornings, me and you
He said, "I love you more"
Now, thinking if everything you said was true

What is true love, asked by me
Hoped you would look in my direction as
answer while sitting near the Christmas tree
She uttered," I don't know about love"
Kissing her, he starts feeling free

Depth and marks or dancing darts
Let's say screeching doesn't help the inner
voice,
Crazy goals don't live without the starts

What is so called success, finally they asked
Dancing haze drama starts living in the raft

Calm Or Not

My calm mind my peaceful heart
Thanks for giving them a head start
Your peaceful voice my naughty toys
My imagination is a piece of art

No heartbeat rush No crazy furs
Should we start taking decisions that are
called smart?
Okay let's think think think and more think
Nah! Let's have fun and play with a shopping
cart

Maybe Melancholic

Melancholic mains treating freaky affairs
Crushing drama trails and fantastic fails
What's up thought with lavender days
Tricky down crazy town down with the haze

People beg and beseech for it with all life
Still, that freaky person keeps throwing it
away

Trying, prying, crying, they tried to stay
But she was resolute to keep everyone at bay

Endeavored to approach and reach trying to
help her thrive
But she was determined to never get to
hierarchical ranks
Fight and Clash, let's win the duel
People love a martyr than a survivor, let's say

Euphoric Stars

I dream of stream while visiting the rain
Searching through the woods, wandering
through the pain
Touched a firefly gazing through the sky
Immense outbursts should not be in vain

Falling water with beautiful stars lane
Magical momentum feeling desolation on the
train
Stilling contemplation gazing at the moon
Quests of passion don't need to explain

Never happened, ever happened, thoughts of
chain
Euphoric leaves and stars to sustain
Listening maroons on an island high
Let's keep all the dreams and ideas from a
refrain

Stop Thinking

I was thinking more and more
People watching returned to the store
Crazy stamps ahead
Meeting her by the road to explore

Light layers with bright chairs
Drama trauma freaky fours
She tried, and he cried the moment finally
dried
Let's be steady and dance some more
I did not see the end of the shore

Christmas lights have been shining since
Twilight
Magical twinkle was being ready to restore
I watched the bliss emerging through the
core
Let's keep dancing till the dawn and before

Misery or Gift

Is it a misery or a gift
Or a different kind of curse to lift
Do you know how it ends
Or is it still a mystery to fit

Rustling winds and creaking sounds
Jack of all trades or another devil to fall
Have you wrapped your head with this around
When was the last time you really felt the ground

You cannot lose when you can choose
So choose if it is a misery or a gift to use
It is a choice of your mindset
Trust the Universe and it'll not let you regret

Fear or Not

As long as I live in secret
Maybe I'll start feeling safe
As long as I live in silence
Maybe I won't feel scared

It has been some almost 18 years
Still haven't overcome that fear
As long as I live in hiding
Maybe I won't feel so terrified

Really a Legend?

The legend of death and life
Have you used yourself a knife
Bruises and markings were not veiled
I did not intend to explain the trail

Despicable cryptic traces were cured
Abandoned my desires and blues that lured
Please let her see the truth that she required
She stopped feeling inspired

The key was her heart and compassion
Tried holding my feelings but still felt tired
She endured and survived with stillness
I hope those emotions don't get fired

She's Just Trying To Live

Am I broken, I don't know
Everyone agrees that I am
I still don't know what's the scam

I try to survive, did not had time to thrive
Everyone stayed in their hives
Thought that I was naive

Oh wait, she's dumb
Did you know that she constantly felt numb

Oh listen, she's a slut
Did you know she tried to drown herself in
the tub

Oh shit, she's here
Did you know what she had to bear
GET LOST YOU DON'T BELONG HERE
You have the personality of Britney Spears
Depression trauma die bitch
She's just trying to live a life here